The Nature and Science of
COLOR

Jane Burton and Kim Taylor

Gareth Stevens Publishing
MILWAUKEE

For a free color catalog describing Gareth Stevens Publishing's list of high-quality books
and multimedia programs, call 1-800-542-2595 (USA) or 1-800-461-9120 (Canada).
Gareth Stevens Publishing's Fax: (414) 225-0377.
See our catalog, too, on the World Wide Web: http://gsinc.com

Library of Congress Cataloging-in-Publication Data

Burton, Jane.
The nature and science of color / by Jane Burton and Kim Taylor.
p. cm. -- (Exploring the science of nature)
Includes index.
Summary: Explains how various colors are produced by reflected light and
briefly discusses the occurrences of colors in nature.
ISBN 0-8368-1940-3 (lib. bdg.)
1. Color--Juvenile literature. 2. Colors--Juvenile literature. [1. Color.] I. Taylor, Kim.
II. Title. III. Series: Burton, Jane. Exploring the science of nature.
QC495.5.B89   1998
535.6--dc21   97-34237

First published in North America in 1998 by
Gareth Stevens Publishing
1555 North RiverCenter Drive, Suite 201
Milwaukee, Wisconsin 53212 USA

This U.S. edition © 1998 by Gareth Stevens, Inc. Created with original © 1997 by White
Cottage Children's Books. Text and photographs © 1998 by Jane Burton and Kim Taylor.
Photographs on pages 11, 22 (right), 23 (left), 24 (right), and 25 are by Mark Taylor.
Conceived, designed and produced by White Cottage Children's Books,
29 Lancaster Park, Richmond, Surrey TW10 6AB, England.
Additional end matter © 1998 by Gareth Stevens, Inc.

The rights of Jane Burton and Kim Taylor to be identified as the authors of this work
have been asserted by them in accordance with the Copyright, Design and Patents
Act 1988. Educational consultant, Jane Weaver; scientific adviser, Dr. Jan Taylor.

Printed in the United States of America

1 2 3 4 5 6 7 8 9 02 01 00 99 98

Contents

Words that appear in the glossary are printed in **boldface** type the first time they occur in the text.

Seeing Color

Red

A rainbow gleams with the purest colors — red, orange, yellow, green, blue, indigo, and violet. The colors merge, one into another. An entire range of different shades exists between the main colors of a rainbow. Our eyes can see them, but we do not have names for these colors.

Orange

Being able to tell the difference between colors is important for many creatures. Birds, for instance, can see food in the form of a caterpillar because the caterpillar is a slightly different shade of green than the leaf on which it sits.

Not all animals can see colors, however. Dogs probably see the world in shades of just one color. Color is not very important to dogs because they rely more on another sense — the sense of smell. This sense is not very well developed in humans.

Yellow

Opposite: A rainbow spans the spray-filled gorge of Victoria Falls on a sunny afternoon in Zimbabwe.

Green

Violet

Indigo

Blue

The Colors of Light

Top: The wings of some yellow butterflies reflect ultraviolet patterns, unseen by humans.

To understand color, you need to understand the nature of light. Light is made of **electromagnetic** waves. These spread out from any light source, such as the Sun, like ripples on the surface of water. Light waves travel at tremendous speed.

The distance between light waves, called **wavelength**, is what determines the color of the light. The longest wavelength of light that humans can see is red. The shortest is violet. **Ultraviolet** has an even shorter wavelength, but humans cannot see it. Only some birds and bees can see it.

In addition, humans cannot see **infrared**, which has a longer wavelength than red light.

Right: Colorless rays of white light shine through the branches of Douglas fir trees on a misty winter's morning.

But humans feel some infrared because infrared is heat. A rattlesnake has special pits on its face that are sensitive to infrared. The snake "sees" the warmth of a mouse's body, even in darkness.

The Sun's rays appear colorless to humans. But, in fact, they contain all the colors of the rainbow mixed together. This mixture is known as white light. When white light strikes a chalk cliff, for instance, the cliff appears white to us because chalk reflects all colors equally. A lump of flint lodged in the chalk absorbs all colors equally and so looks dark gray or even black. Grass growing on the cliff is green because it **reflects** green light and **absorbs** the other colors.

Paintbox Colors

Most of the colors in plants, animals, and minerals are visible due to **pigments**. These are chemical substances that absorb some wavelengths of light, while reflecting others. Colors that we see are the wavelengths that have been reflected. Grass is green because it reflects green light, not because it is itself green. Prove this by shining orange light onto grass. The grass no longer looks green because there is no green light for it to reflect.

The feathers of many birds are colored with pigments. With some birds, the amount of color depends on what the bird eats. Flamingos eat algae and small water animals that contain a pigment that colors their feathers pink.

Many animals and plants produce pigments that are **soluble** in water. Soluble pigments are known as dyes. To defend themselves, sea slugs squirt out a purple dye called gentian violet. The brilliant crimson of a turaco's wing feathers is due to a dye called turacin.

Many of the dyes that color our food and clothing come from plant and animal pigments.

9

The Importance of Green

Top: Beech leaves are bright green when they first open in spring.

Opposite: Moss grows in the cool shade of a damp forest, collecting all the light it can for photosynthesis.

Below: The lettuce sea slug looks like a green leaf. It even undergoes photosynthesis like one. Microscopic particles of green plant material, called **chloroplasts**, in its body make sugars that the sea slug lives on. This animal does not need to eat!

Vast areas of the natural world are green because green is the color of leaves. Green is often thought of as the color of fresh natural growth. But, the fact that nearly all leaves appear green is a result of the process called **photosynthesis**. This process enables plants to use light energy from the Sun to make the sugars they use for growth. Photosynthesis is the basis for nearly all life on Earth. Plants rely on photosynthesis for food. Animals, in turn, rely on the plants.

At the heart of photosynthesis is the green pigment called **chlorophyll**. It absorbs some wavelengths of light and uses the energy to make sugar. But not all wavelengths of light are useful in this process, and chlorophyll reflects these wavelengths. In fact, the color green is *not* needed for photosynthesis, and that is why leaves reflect it. The beautiful green of forests and fields is simply wasted light that plants cannot use.

Iridescent Colors

Top: The wings of a morpho butterfly flash purple and sky blue, depending on how the sunlight "catches" them.

Not all colors are due to pigments. When a beautifully colored soap bubble bursts, it leaves only a drop of clear water. The rainbow colors in a bubble depend on the thickness of the film of water that forms the bubble.

The colors in a rainbow are produced by **refraction**. Each color in white light from the Sun is bent at a slightly different angle by falling raindrops. The raindrops act like thousands of tiny **prisms**. They separate the colors, and we see them as bands of colored light.

Right: A European kingfisher's brilliant blue and turquoise blue colors are produced by very thin layers of **transparent** material on the surface of its feathers. The material reflects the blues and absorbs the other colors.

Left: The iridescent feathers of these purple glossy starlings gleam blue, green, or purple, depending on the angle at which the light strikes them. The colors shimmer over their plumage as the birds move.

The brilliant **iridescent** blues and greens of hummingbirds and kingfishers and of many species of butterflies are due to **interference**. The surface of the feathers of these birds and the scales on the wings of butterflies are built of microscopically thin layers of transparent material. These complicated and very precise layers strongly reflect light of particular wavelengths. Other wavelengths are reflected much less strongly because the layers cause the waves to interfere with one another. In effect, they cancel each other out.

Trying to extract color from a hummingbird's feathers would be as frustrating as trying to collect the colors from a rainbow by holding a jar to catch the raindrops beneath it!

Below: Many iridescent blue scales make up each of the blue flecks on a small tortoiseshell butterfly's wings.

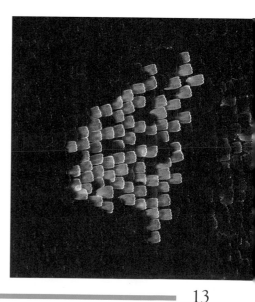

Bright Colors

Top: Plants as well as animals wear bright colors to "advertise" themselves. This pansy advertises itself to bees.

Animals that wear bright colors are like people who wear brightly colored clothing. They are sure to be noticed. But people change their clothing, while many animals wear their bright colors all the time.

Very often, male birds are brightly colored and the females are brown. This is because males and females play different roles when it comes to raising a family. The male's role is to make sure there is enough food in the area around the nest for the parents and their young. To do this, he must chase away other birds of the same species

Below: The golden pheasant male is brilliantly colored. He spends his days strutting through his territory, chasing off other males. . .

while the female golden pheasant is almost invisible sitting on her nest.

that might eat the food. The bright colors of a male act like a painted sign saying, "keep away."

The bright colors of many male birds also attract mates. For instance, brightly colored male birds of paradise dance in front of females, displaying their colors. The male bird of paradise will even pluck leaves from trees so that a shaft of sunlight can fall onto his iridescent feathers. This makes the feathers shimmer in the otherwise dark tropical forest.

Both male and female butterflies can be brightly colored. Their bright color patterns, like those of the bird of paradise, tell other butterflies of the same species that a mate is available.

The strikingly colorful male rock agama lizard *(above)* makes himself even more visible when threatening other males by bobbing his head up and down. The female *(below)* is not as vividly colored.

Below: The small tortoiseshell butterfly has a distinctive color pattern on the upper side of its wings. This pattern is recognized by other butterflies of the same species.

Right: This song thrush feasts on ripe, red currants. Later, the bird will drop the currant seeds far away, helping spread the plant.

Many plants also have bright colors. The colorful flowers in gardens, woods, and fields advertise that they contain **nectar**. You might think the nectar is free for any insect or bird to collect, but it is not. The "price" of the nectar is that insects and birds must carry **pollen** from the flowers on which they feed to other flowers. In this way, pollen from one plant **fertilizes** the seeds of another plant. Seeds cannot grow unless fertilization takes place.

Some flowers reflect ultraviolet patterns that are invisible to humans. But they are visible to bees. The patterns guide bees to the nectar.

Below: Green berries of woody nightshade contain unripe seeds. The green color makes the berries unattractive to birds.

But as the seeds ripen, the berries turn red and succulent — an advertisement to birds to come and eat them.

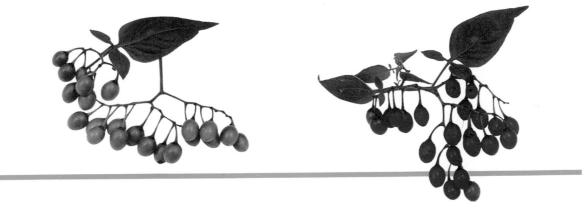

The often vivid colors of ripe fruits and berries attract animals that feed on them. The animals distribute the plants far and wide by spreading seeds in many different locations. Of course, this process does not work if an animal eats the fruits and berries before they ripen. For this reason, unripe fruits are often green. They do not turn a more vivid color until they are ready to be eaten.

Below: A red wattlebird sips nectar from the flowers of a eucalyptus tree. The bird carries pollen on its beak and feathers from tree to tree.

Top: A stinging wasp is recognized by its distinctive color pattern.

In the human world, red signifies danger or warning. In the animal world, black and yellow or black and red are often the danger signals.

Animals that display these warning colors usually sting, are poisonous, or taste unpleasant. Their warning colors act as protection against **predators**. Wasps are vividly striped, and they sting. Birds easily recognize wasps and avoid eating them and getting stung. The coloring is good for both the birds and the wasps.

Moths make tasty meals for insect-eating birds, so most species of moths hide during the day. They come out at night when they cannot be seen by predators. But a few species of moths do fly during the day. Some of these are brightly colored. This tells predators that the moths are poisonous. The warning colors of day-flying

Below: Blister beetles carry a dangerous chemical that burns and blisters a predator's skin. The beetle's bold yellow and black markings warn of the danger.

A harmless jewel beetle mimics the color markings of a blister beetle. Predators heed the warning colors and leave the jewel beetle alone as well.

moths work so well that these moths do not need to dart around quickly like other insects to avoid being eaten. Instead, they travel along slowly for all to see.

Warning colors are such good protection for some insects that other, nonpoisonous, insects developed the same color patterns. When one species of animal copies another, it is called **mimicry**. A mimic uses the same warning colors for its own protection as well.

Above: Blister beetles with red markings are just as dangerous as those with yellow markings. Birds and other predators leave them alone.

Changing Colors

Top: A pop-eyed squid swims at the surface of the water, disguised as the underside of a ripple.

Many animals have developed body coloring that makes them almost invisible against their surroundings. The silvery gray fur of an Arctic fox matches the barren rocks and lichens of its environment. This **camouflage** works well until the winter snows come. Then, to stay camouflaged, the fox **molts** its gray fur and grows a white winter coat to match the snow.

Many kinds of Arctic mammals and birds change color in this way, but growing a new coat is a slow process. For this reason, it does not

Below: A chameleon is able to change color in just a few minutes. When this flap-necked chameleon sleeps at night, it is pale green in color.

At dawn, the chameleon changes to a blotchy dark and light green to match the leaves in its surroundings. It stays still as it warms in the Sun, so movement does not spoil the camouflage.

work for animals that keep moving from one sort of background to another. These animals must change color quickly in order to remain camouflaged. A squid swims near the surface of the sea. The animal is a greenish silver, like the underside of the ripples on the surface of the water. But when a predator approaches, the squid instantly turns dark brown and twists up its arms so it looks like a piece of floating seaweed.

Rapid color change is produced by special cells in the skin called **chromatophores**. These cells contain pigments of various colors and can be expanded or contracted. When the squid turns from silver to brown, its brown chromatophores expand, covering the silver ones.

Above: Three dwarf hamsters share a tree stump in late winter. Two are still in their pale winter coats and blend with the melting snow. The third is in summer brown. This color camouflages the hamster against the fungus-covered wood.

Left: When warmed, this male chameleon creeps into a nearby bush. If there is already another male there, the intruder turns blotchy black and spreads its neck flaps as a threat.

Right: High on a
mountain in North
America, the leaves of
a mountain ash, or
rowan, tree turn from
green to bright yellow.
The ripening berries
turn orange. Leaves
on the surrounding
blueberry bushes turn
a flaming red.

Animals are not the only living things that
change color. Plants change color, too, but more
slowly. Berries change color as they ripen. In
autumn, leaves change from green to red, yellow,
and orange. This happens when chlorophyll in
the leaves breaks down and goes back into the
plant, leaving only red and yellow pigments.

Many flowers also change color as they get
older. They may be yellow when they first open,

Below: Flower heads of the tropical
lantana shrub are dark pink when first
starting to bud. Bees and moths
investigate but, finding no nectar,
soon fly on.

Flowers around the edge of the head
open first. They are bright yellow and
strongly attract nectar-loving insects.

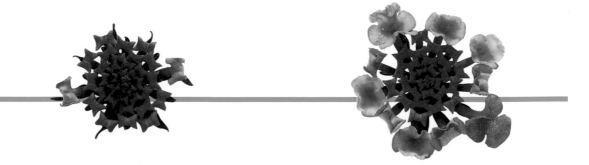

Left: Maples are known for the brilliance of their autumn colors. With the first frosts, the dying leaves turn red, orange, and yellow before falling to the ground.

but then change to red or even purple. These changes send important messages to insects that feed on the flowers.

Insects quickly learn to tell which flowers are newly opened and, therefore, loaded with pollen and nectar. Older flowers that have turned a different shade no longer have much nectar left. These older flowers, however, still add to the show of color.

As more nectar-rich, yellow flowers open, the older, spent flowers turn pale pink. This lets visiting insects know that the nectar in these flowers is exhausted.

The oldest flowers become crimson as they continue to age.

Sky Colors

The surface of Earth is multi-colored. It contains green leaves, red flowers and berries, blue waters, brilliantly varied butterflies and birds, and much, much more.

The sky undergoes regular changes in color. During the day, it normally appears blue, and the clouds are white or gray. At sunrise and sunset, there can be a show of red, orange, and gold.

Top: On a cloudy evening, the Sun sets as a fiery orange ball.

Above: During a sunset, the sky in the west flames red, orange, and gold. Dust and smoke in the air filter out the other colors.

Right: Over desert dunes, the cloudless sky appears a deep blue. In blazing sunshine, Earth's colors become their most intense.

On a cloudless day, the daytime sky appears blue because blue light is scattered by Earth's **atmosphere**. Imagine rays of light coming from the Sun. The rays contain light of all wavelengths — red, orange, yellow, green, blue, and so on. Most of this light passes straight through the atmosphere and reaches Earth unchanged. But blue light, which has a short wavelength, bounces off **molecules** of oxygen and water in the atmosphere. This bounced or scattered blue light is what we see in the sky.

Above: On a cloudy day, this sky appears gray, with darker gray reflections on the ruffled surface of the river. The colors of the trees are muted, and even the white snow seems pale.

Ocean Depths

Top: The yellow of this golden seahorse would look green if it swam into deeper water.

Seawater absorbs red and yellow light quickly, making the water appear greenish blue. Blue light penetrates much deeper in water than other colors. But eventually, all the blue is absorbed, too, and darkness reigns in the depths.

At depths where only blue light penetrates, everything appears a dull gray-blue. But when a diver shines a flashlight, vivid colors unfold. Red, orange, blue, and yellow fish swim through brilliantly colored corals. Light from the flashlight has to travel just a short distance to reach them, making true colors visible again.

The colors that appear depend as much on the color of the light that is shining on them as on pigment. True colors can only be seen in white light.

Opposite: A shoal of gray mullet fish swims in the ocean depths. Their silvery sides reflect the blueness of the under-sea world. Beadlet anemones appear purple or pale gray-green in the blue light. Out of the water, they are bright red and apple green.

Left: Even in deep water, butterfly fish show their true colors when lit by flashlight.

27

Activities:

The Magic of Color

Color plays all kinds of tricks on the eye. The color you see in any object depends on many things — such as the nature of the light falling on the object and what other colors are near it. The color you see may even depend on what colors you have been looking at immediately beforehand. You can test this last effect by staring with one eye through a piece of brightly colored plastic for a minute or so. Now take the plastic away, and look at any scene — first with one eye and then the other.

Compare the colors you see with each eye. If the plastic is red, for instance, the eye that was covered by it sees its **complementary color**, which is green. The scene viewed through this eye, compared to the other, appears abnormally green.

Similarly, orange plastic will produce a scene in a complementary blue. In effect, your eye tries to compensate for seeing too much of one color by adding some of that color's complementary color.

Next-door Neighbors
The effect colors have on each other when they are close together can also be tested. For this experiment, you will need some brightly colored paints (poster colors or acrylics), paintbrushes, white paper, a pencil, and a ruler.

With the pencil and ruler, draw three squares on one sheet of paper, each with sides of 4 inches (100 millimeters). In the middle of each square, draw another square with 1.5-inch (40-mm) sides. Carefully paint all three small inner squares an identical navy blue. Then paint each of the remaining larger squares a different color, such as red, yellow, or green.

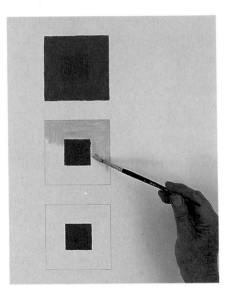

When the paint is dry, study the effect one color has on another. You know that the small squares are all the same shade of blue because you used the same paint on them. Yet, they no longer look the same. The shade of blue in the small squares has been affected by the color next to it. Of course, this is not a real effect. It is an illusion, or trick. Some artists purposely use this effect in their paintings.

More tricks are in store for you if you repeat the experiment. Each time you do the experiment, use a different color for the small squares.

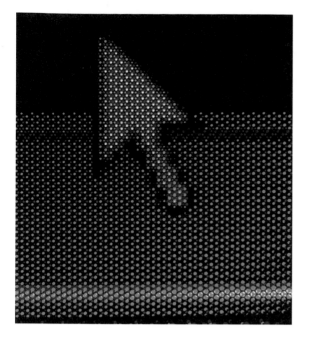

areas of the screen. There, the three primary colors are at their brightest. In black areas of the screen, the dots may be so dim that you can hardly see them *(left)*.

Now place the magnifying glass over a colorful picture in this book. It, too, is made up of dots of three primary colors together with black. But instead of red, green, and blue, the primaries in printing are red, yellow, and blue. The difference between a printed page and a color television screen is that, in printing, the dots may overlap. For instance, a blue and a yellow dot, printed on top of each other, make a green dot. By varying the size of these primary-colored dots on the page or their brightness on a television screen, it is possible to make many thousands, even millions, of different color shades.

Below: When complementary colors are placed side by side, each color looks stronger. The rich red of these poppies stands out boldly against the lush complementary green of the leaves.

White Light

It is difficult to understand how mixing all the colors of the rainbow together can make white light — especially when mixing all the colors in a paintbox just produces a drab brown. The fact is — colored light and pigments work quite differently from one another. Pigments only reflect the light that falls on them, whereas light itself is the true source of all color.

Not all the colors of the rainbow are needed to make white. In fact, just three will do. These are red, green, and blue and are known as **primary colors** of light.

To see how just three colors can produce any imaginable color, you need a magnifying glass and a working color television or computer screen. With the magnifying glass, study the screen closely and observe that the picture is made up of dots or lines. Look particularly at white

Glossary

absorb: to soak up.

atmosphere: the layer of air and clouds that surrounds Earth.

camouflage: patterns of color on an animal or object that make it difficult for the animal or object to be seen.

chlorophyll: a green substance in plants that absorbs the energy found in sunlight and turns it into energy-rich food.

chloroplasts: tiny, round bodies containing chlorophyll that are found in the cells of plants and some animals.

chromatophores: special cells in an animal's skin that control the animal's color.

complementary colors: a pair of colors, each of which reflects all the wavelengths of light absorbed by the other.

electromagnetic wave: the form in which heat, light, and other kinds of energy travel through space.

fertilize: to cause a male cell to join with a female cell.

infrared: radiation with a wavelength that is longer than red light. Heat is infrared radiation.

interference: the effect produced when two sets of light waves (or other types of waves) of the same frequency mix together so that they either support or cancel each other out.

iridescent: brilliant, shiny colors produced by interference.

mimicry: the copying of appearance, sounds, or smells.

molecule: the smallest part of a substance, made up of two or more atoms joined together.

molt: to shed skin, feathers, or fur.

nectar: the sweet liquid produced by flowers that attracts bees, birds, and other animals.

photosynthesis: the process in which plants use energy from the Sun to make food.

pigment: the coloring matter found in inks and paints. Natural pigments occur in plants and animals.

pollen: grains, usually yellow, in a flower that fertilize the female part of the flower.

predator: an animal that hunts other animals for food.

primary colors: a group of three colors that cannot be made from any other colors.

prism: a piece of glass, a raindrop, or another transparent material that refracts light into the colors of the rainbow.

reflect: to send back light rays, heat, or sound from a surface.

refraction: the bending of light from a straight path.

soluble: when a substance is able to mix completely with a liquid.

transparent: a feature of a substance that permits the passage of light without scattering the light.

ultraviolet: invisible radiation that has a wavelength shorter than violet light.

wavelength: the distance between waves.

Plants and Animals

The common names of plants and animals vary from language to language. But plants and animals also have scientific names, based on Greek or Latin words, that are the same the world over. Each plant and animal has two scientific names. The first name is called the genus. It starts with a capital letter. The second name is the species name. It starts with a small letter.

beadlet anemone (*Actinea equina*) — North Atlantic shores 26-27

Douglas fir (*Pseudotsuga douglasii*) — western North America, planted elsewhere 6

flap-necked chameleon (*Chamaeleo dilepis*) — southern Africa 20-21

golden butterflyfish (*Chaetodon auriga*), **checkered butterflyfish** (*Chaetodon chrysurus*), and **rainbow butterflyfish** (*Chaetodon trifasciatus*) — tropical seas 27

golden pheasant (*Chrysolophus pictus*) — China, kept worldwide 14

golden seahorse (*Hippocampus kuda*) — Indo-Pacific Ocean cover, 27

gray mullet (*Mulgil labrosus*) — northeastern Atlantic 26-27

greater flamingo (*Phoenicopterus ruber*) — Africa, India, southern Europe 8-9

kingfisher (*Alcedo atthis*) — Europe 12

lantana (*Lantana camara*) — Brazil, warm countries worldwide 22-23

lettuce sea slug (*Elysia crispata*) — Indo-Pacific Ocean 10

a moss (*Hylocomium splendens*) — North America 10

Namibian rock agama (*Agama planiceps*) — southwestern Africa 15

purple glossy starling (*Lamprotornis purpurea*) — western and eastern Africa 13

red wattlebird (*Anthocaera carunculata*) — Western Australia 17

Ross's turaco (*Mussophaga violacea*) — central Africa 9

song thrush (*Turdus philomelos*) — Europe, Asia, northern Africa 16

western diamond-back rattlesnake (*Crotalus atrox*) — North America 7

woody nightshade (*Solanum dulcamara*) — Europe, Asia 16

Books to Read

Color and Light. Hands on Science (series). (Gareth Stevens)

Exploring Light. Ed Catherall (Raintree)

Light. Neil Ardley (Simon & Schuster)

Light. Rae Bains (Troll Associates)

Light. David Burnie (Dorling Kindersley)

Light and Color. Gary Gibson (Copper Beech Books)

Projects With Color and Light. Simple Science Projects (series). John Williams (Gareth Stevens)

What's the Difference Between . . . Lenses and Prisms and Other Scientific Things? Gary Soucie (John Wiley)

Why are Zebras Black and White? Terry Martin (Dorling Kindersley)

Videos and Web Sites

Videos

Color: A First Film. (Phoenix/BFA)
Color From Light. (Churchill)
Exploring Light and Color.
  (United Learning)
How Light Changes Color. (Films for the
  Humanities and Sciences)
What Is Color? (Encyclopædia Britannica
  Educational Corporation)
What's In A Rainbow? (Journal Films)

Web Sites

www.unidata.ucar.edu/staff/blynds/
  rnbw.html
photoscience.la.asu.edu/photosyn/
  education/learn.html
photoscience.la.asu.edu/photosyn/
  study.html
www.cea.berkeley.edu/Education/light/
  light_tour.html

Index